KILLING IT

THE ACTION GIRL'S GUIDE TO SAVING THE WORLD...
WHILE LOOKING HOT!

JOAN FORD

THE DEVASTATOR

WRITTEN BY
JOAN FORD

DESIGN
MIKE REDDY

FRONT COVER & CHAPTER ART
SPENCER DINA

INTERIOR SPOT ART
MIKE REDDY & JOHN MATHIAS

EDITORS
AMANDA MEADOWS & GEOFFREY GOLDEN

ISBN-10: 1-942099-10-X

ISBN-13: 978-1-942099-10-9

First Edition: June 2016

devastatorpress.com

PRINTED IN ~~B.U.G. FORCE HEADQUARTERS~~ KOREA

"WE CAN DISCUSS SEXISM IN
SURVIVAL SITUATIONS WHEN I GET BACK."
—DR. ELLIE SATTLER, *JURASSIC PARK*

INTRODUCTION

o, you want to be an Action Girl? You've spent years turning your body and mind into finely tuned instruments of pure destruction, and now you're ready to unleash your inner "strong female character?" Well, hold up. You may have the "strong" part down, but we gotta work on the "female."

Hey! My name is Joan Havok. I'm an agent for The Knight's Guard, a top secret global defense agency, and for years I've been walking that razor-thin line between woman and warrior. I've learned how to dismantle a bomb without breaking a nail, how to outrun a fireball without breaking a heel and how to fight alongside the big boys without breaking any of the thousands of social contracts that dictate how men and women should act at all times.

Figuring all this out wasn't easy. No one gave me a flash drive full of schematics about how to survive as a lady in today's crazy modern world. Wesley down in the tech department never built me a quantum, stealth cloak to make me invisible in embarrassing social situations. And Admiral Zorn taught me seventeen ways to kill a man, but could he tell me how soon to text a guy after a first date? NOPE!

That's why I need to share all this stuff with you. (The "how to be a girl" stuff! I'm sure you already know plenty of ways to kill a man.) I wanted to create the definitive guidebook for all the aspiring Action Girls out there. And yeah, I know what you're thinking: *Joan, isn't it wildly sexist to imply that if someone follows a bunch of arbitrary rules she'll be more of a girl than someone who doesn't? Isn't the whole premise of this book wildly problematic?*

SHUT UP!

The only problem with this book is that you're overthinking it. The worst thing you can do on any mission is overthink it.

If you take the advice in the pages that follow, you won't have to think about anything anymore. Every situation or scenario you could ever encounter as a woman will be thoroughly covered in this eighty page illustrated book. It's all the stuff we were too embarrassed to ask our moms, and also you couldn't because your mother was murdered in her laboratory when you were only seven by a Russian assassin screaming, "WHERE IS IT? WHERE IS THE KRATOS SERUM?" (If only my scientist mother had told me what the Kratos Serum was when she was giving me all those injections as a child...)

So don't stress, and don't sweat... 'cause your makeup will run if you start sweating. Being an Action Girl can be hard, it can be confusing, and sometimes it can make you want to throw up your hands and let the Brotherhood of S.T.A.B succeed in overthrowing all of the world's governments. But if you follow my lead, you'll be Killing It!

JOAN HAVOK

CROSS MY HEART
AND T.R.O.P.E. TO DIE

Let's get one thing straight ladies: the goal of this book isn't to force you into some kind of box. (We're Action Girls. The only boxes that can hold us are made of triple-reinforced unobtainium.) Each and every one of you reading this right now is your own, unique woman warrior. You're fierce, you're independent, and you've got your own special set of skills to help save the day. With all that amazingness, there could never be just one "type of woman."

There are actually seven types of women. Exactly seven. Every single one of you reading this right now fits into one of seven, pre-existing personality types, or T.R.O.P.E.S. (Tightly Regulated Optimized Personality Efficiency Signifiers) as I like to call them.

Deciphering your T.R.O.P.E. is soooooooo important. Once you know it, you can start altering yourself to match it verbatim. You'll know which traits to hold onto, and which traits to hack off like a limb infected by the Inferno Virus. Action Girls always cut to the chase, so you don't want people to waste their time getting to know your highly nuanced personality. You want people to take one look and say, "Oh yeah, I get what her deal is."

So what *is* your deal? What is your T.R.O.P.E.?

T.R.O.P.E. #1: *THE GOSH GIRL*

Gosh Girls don't go looking for action... action comes looking for them. They're the girl next door thrust into an adventure. But no matter what form adventure takes you'll be ready to bumble through it with a purse full of random shit that becomes incredibly useful at the most unlikely moments.

A Gosh Girl is always saying things like "GOSH! How did I get mixed up in all this?" or, "A GUN?! YOU WANT ME TO SHOOT A GUN?! I CAN BARELY SHOOT A PICTURE WITH MY iPHONE!" and while you're saying all that you're waving your arms around, and you accidentally shoot the bad guy that was creeping up on you.

TACTICAL ADVANTAGE: No skills! Gosh Girls are absolutely unequipped for the missions they get thrust into, which is totally cute. Everyone will find you adorable.

TACTICAL LIABILITY: No skills! While adorable, having no tactical experience will also increase your chances of getting murdered by one thousand percent. Plus your favorite dress is totally going to get ruined. (Just try getting blood out of charmeuse silk!)

Tragedy Magnets (or Trag Mags) have given up everything — family, romance, children — to pursue a life of bloodshed, brutality and emotional isolation. They're the ultimate career gals!

These independent ladies have all been emotionally crippled in some seriously exciting ways. Whether you've been brainwashed by a secret government agency, dedicated your life to finding your parent's killers, or you just love the rush of seeing someone bleed out from an expertly administered knife wound, all Trag Mags have one thing in common: no matter how far they run they'll never be able to escape... themselves. And why would they want to, when every day is another non-stop thrill ride of existential terror and moral ambiguity?!

TACTICAL ADVANTAGE: Tragic backstory! The heartbreaking circumstances of your life will make a perfect icebreaker when talking to any guy.

TACTICAL LIABILITY: PTSD, as in Post Traumatic SEX Disorder! Your violent tendencies may take over in the heat of passion. Be careful not to crush your lover's spine with your thighs... again. (But if you do, it's not like you've never disposed of a dead body before!)

T.R.O.P.E. #3: *WAIFISH WARRIOR*

Waifish Warrior may look like a varsity cheerleader with a horrible eating disorder, but beneath her slight frame, small stature and calcium-deficient bones lies enough raw strength to punch a three-hundred-pound trucker through a cement wall.

Just remember, a Waifish Warrior always inherits her absurd strength from some insane external force, like an alien amulet, demon amulet, or top secret government NanoAmulet! That way men can marvel at your abilities while remaining confident that there's no way you could have achieved them on your own!

TACTICAL ADVANTAGE: Easy money! Waifish Warriors are never short on cash thanks to the abundance of arm wrestling contests and drinking competitions happening at local trucker bars.

TACTICAL LIABILITY: Metaphors! Almost everything that ever happens to you will be some sort of metaphor for womanhood. Just once it would be awesome to fight a vampire army that wasn't a physical manifestation of the wage gap!

A Tech Escort can save the world with nothing more than a few lines of code and nanowave-enhanced laptop with unlimited mainframe access. (A laptop with no nanowave enhancements will NOT work!) They're like the Action Girl geek squad, only they're qualified to do their jobs and you can tolerate looking at them.

How do they control the entire world's technological infrastructure from a dimly lit, computer station? Who cares! They'd much rather talk about their fave EDM band, or their current shade of pink hair dye. Tech Escorts are the quirkiest Action Girls because, let's face it: if a girl is into computers, then the rest of her personality must be pretty weird too.

TACTICAL ADVANTAGE: Dirty tech! Flirting comes easy to Tech Escorts since almost anything computer-related can be turned into a double entendre, what with all the uploading and downloading and such.

TACTICAL LIABILITY: Skin cancer! Studies have discovered that the number one cause of Non-Hodgkin's Lymphoma is sitting in front of a computer screen that rear projects green text-code onto your face.

010101
101101
010101
101101

101101
010101

T.R.O.P.E. #5: *EXOTIC*

Exotic Action Girls are Asian. I'd keep going, but that's pretty much it. Maybe they're Icelandic every once in a while?

TACTICAL ADVANTAGE: Martial arts, probably.

TACTICAL LIABILITY: Doing stuff that's not martial arts.

Boss Ladies run the show. They're supervising this task force, managing this agency and are responsible for the lives of everyone in this entire company... so they don't have time for any of your bullshit. They're the Action Girls who have been promoted to positions of power, and they know the best way to wield that power is by never letting anybody have any fun. Good luck trying out some kind of risky stunt or untested maneuver when one of these control freaks is around.

Some might think of them as nothing more than a bunch of humorless, stone-faced bitches. But their humorless, stone bitch faces are just masks! Every Boss Lady secretly wants to be defied by some renegade young agent trying out the riskiest, untested maneuver they've ever seen.

TACTICAL ADVANTAGE: Badges! Boss Ladies have confiscated hundreds of badges from misbehaving male agents. Now they have all the badges!

TACTICAL LIABILITY: Always wrong! There will literally never be a time that their insistence on doing things by the book turns out to be correct. Doing things by the book will always be the wrong move.

T.R.O.P.E. #7: *ENEMY FINE*

Say hello to Enemy Fine. And while you're at it, say goodbye too, because she's about to pull the trigger on that silencer pistol she's got pressed to the back of your skull. Enemy Fines are Action Girls *gone bad*! They've pledged their allegiance to the United States of Anarchy, or maybe the British Commonwealth of Treachery, or sometimes even the Cybernetic Sovereign Republic of Robo-France. (Ugh... remember when that computer took over France?)

These duplicitous divas use their own bodies as deadly weapons. It's the bait they use to lure men to their doom. They have no shame in flaunting their sexuality to get what they want (and not in the cool, empowering way all the other T.R.O.P.E.S. do).

TACTICAL ADVANTAGE: Sexual experimentation! Congratulations, you're the only Action Girl who is allowed to be anything other than one hundred percent heterosexual. Kiss a lady sometime, if you feel like it!

TACTICAL LIABILITY: Sad death! When you die it will always be in a sad, prolonged fashion so a male hero can watch with tears in his eyes and wonder, "Why couldn't I have saved her?"

I know I said there were only seven
T.R.O.P.E.S., but get ready for a mind blowing
twist... I was lying! There's actually an
exceedingly rare eighth T.R.O.P.E., one that
can't be classified because... get ready
for another mind blowing twist... it's me!
That's right, me! Joan Havok! I'm the eighth
T.R.O.P.E. I don't fit into a single category... I
fit into two! I have a dark past but I'm also
superhumanly strong. So complex!

Don't feel bad that you can't be complex
like me. I've just always been like this, ever
since Admiral Zorn recruited me for the
Knight's Guard Academy after my scientist
mother was murdered and her laboratory
mysteriously exploded for some reason.
Now I won't rest until I've unraveled the
mystery of who killed my scientist mother
and what was this "Kratos Serum" she was
working on. Hopefully my superhuman
strength and agility will help lead me to the
answer one day!

GO FOR THE SKILL!
**BITCH
SWITCH:**
The ability to switch from
super bitchy to super
vulnerable at a
moment's notice.

BITCH
CHILL

QUIZ: WHAT'S YOUR T.R.O.P.E.?

Time for the best part of any self-help book: a rigorous eight-question quiz that will make you feel like you're actually accomplishing something!

1. The word that best describes me is...

A) Bumbling

B) Seething

C) Asian (You can stop taking quiz if this is your answer.)

2. The best way to kill a man is...

A) With a remote detonator fifty miles away.

B) Uppercutting him through a warehouse ceiling.

C) Emasculating him until his penis falls off.

3. My spirit animal is...

A) The praying mantis, haunted by all the mates she's killed.

B) The praying mantis, with a trophy room full of her dead mates.

C) Pray-Pray, the sassy hacker mantis from B.U.G. Force.

4. If I could be a member of any team it would be...

A) Crime Stoppers International

B) Monster Killers Local 572

C) B.U.G. Force

5. If I had to infiltrate a heavily guarded hideout I would...

A) Flip over all the security lasers.

B) Sex it up big time with all the guards.

C) Crawl through the air ducts because I'm a tiny little bug.

6. The first quality I look for in a teammate is...

A) Loyalty.

B) A sense of humor.

C) Titanium reinforced spinnerets.

7. My training montage song is...

A) Hearts of Fire

B) Push It to the Limit

C) Bugs Never Say Squish! (Theme from B.U.G. Force)

8. If the world was going to end tomorrow I would...

A) Not let that happen.

B) Not on my watch.

C) Think again, Baron Von Thorax! Your little cockroach utopia is finished. You may be able to survive a nuclear blast, but you're not going to survive B.U.G. Force, because bugs never say SQUISH!

RESULTS: **We'll need to send this to the tech lab for further analysis. Please upload a twelve-point encryption copy of your exam to the dark web for one of our agents to intercept.**

DRESS CODE
OF THE ASSASSIN

Every Action Girl needs a wardrobe full of killer clothes she won't get killed in. Trust me, when Forever 21 tells you that their crop tops will "keep you cool when things get hot," that doesn't mean they're flamethrower-retardant. (I don't even want to tell you how many of my girlfriends have burned to death wearing Cool Breeze Yoga Pants.)

Turning to your R & D department doesn't bear better results. Wesley down in the tech lab can design a new synthetic polymer that repels bullets, lasers, shrapnel, fire and Stage 4 radiation poisoning, but you know what else it repels? MEN! You're never going to catch anyone's eye with your body hidden behind six inches of ugly, gray life-saving fabric.

Bottom line: the only person an Action Girl can rely on when it comes to fashion is her own damn self! When the world gives her lemons, she needs to transform them into Lululemon-inspired spy gear. I'm talking about a little DIY ingenuity, ladies! That's all it takes to turn your LBD into a WMD and transform your clunkiest combat armor into heavy duty haute couture.

To prove my point, I'm giving you a glimpse into my very own closet (don't judge the mess! The last professional closet organizer I hired turned out to be an undercover S.T.A.B. agent.) You'll get a look at four of my favorite outfits that I altered all on my own, along with a guide to how I achieved each look. Just remember to keep these tips top secret. We wouldn't want the bad guys looking *this* good... or continuing to live.

THE ITEM: KNIGHT'S GUARD BATTLE ARMOR

THE MISSION: **It was my first mission as a full-fledged Knight's Guard agent. My squad was being air-dropped into a heavily guarded S.T.A.B. compound to rescue a kidnapped Ukrainian physicist, and of course they assign me this agonizingly androgynous armor for the job. I mean, just look at it! You have no idea what the person wearing it is packing... between their legs! I did not get into this business just so everyone could start ignoring my gender. No way I was going to make my big Action Girl debut looking like some sort of high tech Tilda Swinton.**

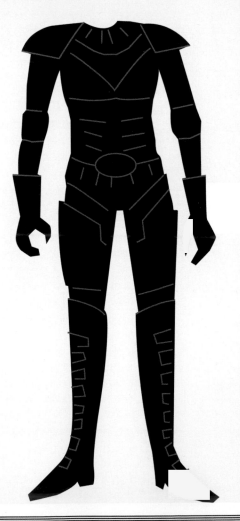

THE RESULT: *BATTLE-KINI*

THE MODIFICATION: **All it took was a few hours with a buzz saw and a soldering iron, and I was able to strip this asexual armor down into a far more feminine form. Sure, some major life support systems had to be sacrificed to make it work. But just look at that promiscuously unprotected breastplate and tell me it wasn't worth lowering my chances of survival just a little bit.**

FIELD EFFECTIVENESS: **The new and improved body armor was a sexy success! The reduced weight made movement a joy, allowing me to break away from my squad who all got murdered by booby traps I triggered (hey... if you can't keep up...). Plus, putting my Action Girl assets on display not only boosted my confidence, but it scored me a date with that Ukrainian Physicist who turned out to be totally hot!**

THE ITEM: BALL GOWN

THE MISSION: **A rogue South African biochemist had stolen the last un-destroyed sample of the Inferno Virus and he was going to hand it off to a S.T.A.B. agent at the Rose Ball in Monte Carlo! I was tasked with seducing the chemist and pocketing the virus before he could make the exchange. I needed to look amazing if I was going to crash the party without an invite, and this two million dollar Christian Dior ball gown was my ticket in!**

Unfortunately, it didn't come with a ticket out! Admiral Zorn had a team of agents in place waiting to extract me once I had the virus, but I was not about to end such an elegant evening being escorted away by a bunch of babysitters. A dress like this deserves a more dramatic exit...

THE MODIFICATION: **By widening the waistline, expanding the skirt train and removing the petticoat, I was able to make enough room under the dress to install a personalized jet repulsor system. Easily achievable with a sewing machine, a little extra fabric and few favors from Wesley down in the tech lab. (Seriously, Wesley is the best! Such a good friend!)**

FIELD EFFECTIVENESS: **Once I had the biochemist out on the dance floor, I activated the repulsor jets and took off through the glass ceiling. The people in my immediate vicinity were vaporized, but the people who were only burned horribly got a goodbye they'll never forget. Admiral Zorn was upset that I destroyed a two-million-dollar piece of Knight's Guard property, but he's a guy. He doesn't understand that some dresses were only meant to be worn once. Plus I got a date with that totally cute South African biochemist! He was just exchanging the virus for his kidnapped daughter! So adorbs!**

THE ITEM: *THE STAFF OF ABRAXAS*

THE MISSION: **This ugly-ass accessory was from my brief stint in the Knight's Guard Supernatural Defense Department. Full disclosure: I hate supernatural missions. It's the sewer maintenance of the action world, and the fashion is horrendous. I've never met a protective shroud or enchanted cloak that didn't make me look totally dumpy. Anyway, the Brides of Abraxas had opened a portal to the underworld with the President's blood and blah, blah, blah... bored yet? Point is, there was a giant snake-demon eating people and the gems in this staff were the only thing that could send it back to hell. But come on, I wasn't about to be seen running around with that tacky thing. The Staff of Abraxas needed some brand new enchantments, and the magic words were "COMPLETE MAKEOVER!"**

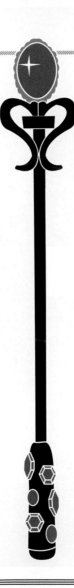

THE RESULT: *PERSONALIZED JEAN JACKET*

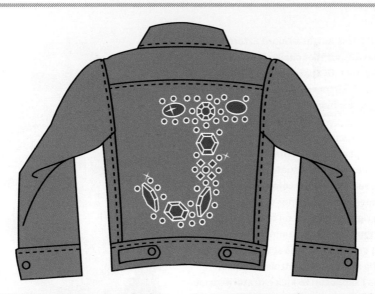

THE MODIFICATION: **If I had to go slumming into the supernatural, I figure why not have fun with it! A magically bedazzled jean jacket struck just the right balance between trashy and glam. Breaking the gems off the staff was easy; all it took was a few magic siphoning spells. But applying them the proved tricky. Hot glue guns and seven thousand-year-old enchanted metals are not natural BFFs.**

FIELD EFFECTIVENESS: **I still break out this jacket when I hit up a local dive bar or get dragged to a casual mummy fight. The downside? Apparently the Abraxas mission was more time-sensitive than I realized, and now there's a snake demon battling God for control of Heaven. *Oh well!* Dealing with the occasional loss is a lesson every Action Girl must learn. That said, I can't feel like a *complete* loser after scoring a date with the totally cute British demonologist I met on the mission!**

THE ITEM: EXTERMINATOR-MECH

THE MISSION: **This Knight's Guard Exterminator Mech was my outfit of choice for my first trip off-planet, to Space Colony Europa Prime. Just a simple clean up mission (acid-spewing space bug infestation, you know the drill), but it was still like a mini-vacay for me and I wanted to look good.**

At first glance, I loved this mech suit. Simple lines that accentuated my slender figure, a red and yellow color scheme that complemented my summer complexion, and just the right amount of on board weaponry to look tough while remaining tasteful. Then I tried it on... UGH! I guess someone decided to set the navigation controls to BASIC. How was I supposed to kick extraterrestrial insect ass when I felt stiffer than a lesbian lumberjack on Oxycodone? It was time to give this baby a fierceness upgrade.

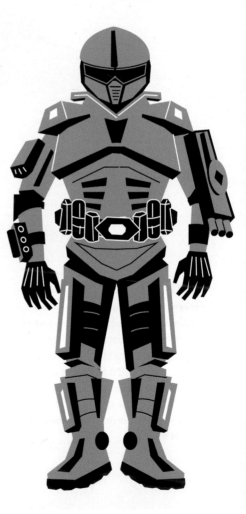

THE RESULT: STOMP ENHANCED EX-MECH

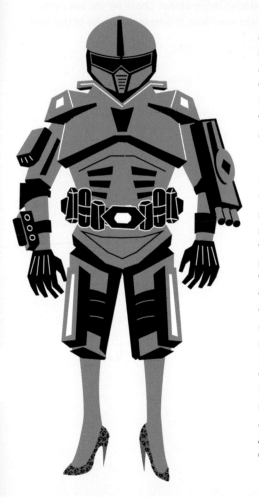

THE MODIFICATION: **Sometimes all it takes to elevate an outfit is a screaming pair of heels. They bring out the boldness within, even in an eight-and-a-half-foot-tall weaponized mech suit. To achieve that runway stomp, I simply grafted on a set of titanium stilettos and touched them up with a pink, leopard print paint job.**

FIELD EFFECTIVENESS: **The new heels really made a statement, and that statement was "CRUNCH" (that's the sound a xentrapede skull makes when you drive a titanium stiletto through it)! I was traipsing through those basic bugs like I was the star of a squishy guts-covered New York Fashion Week. If anything, they worked too well. It turns out the heels increased the mech suit's vertical leap, while doubling as an extremely effective melee weapon. Wesley in the tech department started equipping all of the mech suits with them because he said they were such a great idea. Don't you just hate it when everyone starts copying your look? But I guess it's the price you pay for being an Action Girl trendsetter. (Note: This was an American Space colony, so no cute scientists. Only foreign scientists are cute.)**

CHECK LIST: *ACTION GIRL ESSENTIALS*

There are a few items every Action Girl should have in her closet. Check off the ones you have and buy the ones you don't! Buy them right now! Also, maybe buy doubles of the stuff you do have! Buy stuff to look pretty!

☐ Little Black Dress *(tasteful)*

☐ Little Black Dress *(slutty – for sexy, sex club missions)*

☐ Mini Skirt *(short enough so you can access the gun hidden in your crotch)*

☐ Crotch Gun

☐ Boob Gun *(crotch gun for boobs)*

☐ Boob Gun Accessible Top

☐ Skintight Black Catsuit

☐ Six-Inch Heels

☐ Five-Inch Heels *(for running)*

☐ Samurai Sword Taken from Your Fallen Master

☐ Samurai Sword Taken from Your Fallen Enemy

☐ Samurai Sword Taken from That
   Cool Sword Store at the Mall

☐ That Spray, That Like, Reveals Lasers
   When You Spray It... What Is That Stuff Called?

☐ Towel That Will Stay on During
   Post-Shower Gunfights

☐ Black Bra and Panties (for sleeping)

☐ A Paper Clip, 32 Feet of Steel Knit Fiber,
   a Stopwatch and a Tooth from a Bramble Shark
   (you'll know when the time comes)

☐ Locket with the Coordinates of the
   Delta Zone Hidden Inside

GO FOR THE SKILL!

FACE/SOFT:
The ability to keep your
face perfectly made up and
feminized in even the
most intense
action situations.

RENT OR DIE

When you're an Action Girl, finding a place to live can feel like one big, unwinnable battle. Just try getting a realtor to return your calls when your last three foster homes exploded! No matter how creatively you word it on a rental application, it's gonna set off red flags. And credit scores? How would I have a credit score when I don't have a social security number, fingerprints or any memory of what happened to me between my 16th and 18th birthdays? (Don't worry. Admiral Zorn assures me that's standard for all Knight's Guard recruits.)

But you can't give up. You deserve a sanctuary. A nice, quiet place you can come home to after a long day of government-sanctioned murder. A place where you can kick off your heels, wash off the blood, and slowly sip a glass of red wine while you stare off into the distance in your underwear.

Remember, you're not normal – you're an Action Girl! You gave up normal a long time ago. Do you think I wanted to live in an abandoned warehouse out on the waterfront? It's not exactly my girlhood dream home. But I'm sure glad I do, every time I jump out the window to avoid an explosion and land in the river all safe, sound, sexy and wet.

Action Girls need Action Homes! It's advice I've given to a ton of my girlfriends, and the ones who have taken it have been living pretty ever since. In fact, why don't I introduce you to some of them right now?

FILE #1

NAME: **ST-8C**

(I nicknamed her Stacy! Isn't it crazy how that completely random string of numbers and letters sounds like "Stacy?")

OCCUPATION: **Bioengineered Human Weapon**

HOUSING CRISIS: I met Stacy when she was breaking out from the Bio-Pod in the laboratory where she was being grown. Like so many other one-year-old clones rapidly aged to maturity by government scientists, Stacy was aching for a little bit of independence. She wanted her own apartment!

Well, that's when I had to jump in and pump the brakes. Stacy had never lived by herself before. She had never paid a utility bill, done her laundry, or prepared a meal more complicated than failed clones ground into a nutrient-heavy mush and force-fed via tube. She needed a smaller, starter place where she could really get used to being on her own before she was overwhelmed by the responsibilities of the real world. Luckily, I had the solution...

HER PERFECT PLACE: **A Cryo-Tube!**

Stacy's new Cryo-Tube gave her a ton of room to stretch out and float around naked while still regulating her breathing, eating, and all the other vital life functions that she wasn't ready to do on her own. And the steroid-enriched fluid absorbed through her skin was a way tastier alternative to that bland old clone mush she had been eating. It was exactly the first small step she needed to ease into independence.

WANT MORE PROOF? Talk to any of the other girls who escaped from the clone facility. They all went on stress induced killing sprees. It wasn't long before the government rounded them up, took them back to the lab, and ground them into clone mush. (UGH! Is there anything more embarrassing than having to move back home?)

FINISHING TOUCH: Wires! Every Cryo-Tube needs a bunch of tastefully arranged wires hooked to your body. They'll float in front of your private parts, obscuring them for anyone who unexpectedly pops by for a visit. Plus they connect you to all those awesome life support systems (a must when you're living suspended in liquid)!

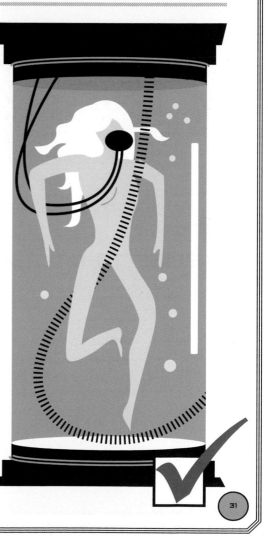

FILE #2

NAME: **BERETTA KALASHNIKOV**

OCCUPATION: **Ex S.T.A.B. Agent**

HOUSING CRISIS: I let Beretta crash with me when she was getting out of a bad relationship with the S.T.A.B. (Strategic Terror Agency of Berlin – funny story, they formed in Moscow but moved to Berlin when they came up with the name.) Now, I'm always happy to see a girl defect from an evil, rogue government agency that isn't treating her like the queen that she is, but it's like she had never heard of Action Girl Break Up Rule Number One:

the amount of time it takes to get over your ex-agency should be equal to one half the number of people you killed while working for that agency. Beretta was taking way longer than that!

It was seriously time for her to move on! She needed a new place to start this new chapter in her life and I was going to make sure she found it before I had to spend one more night listening to her weep herself to sleep singing sad Russian lullabies.

HER PERFECT PLACE: **A barely furnished apartment**
Barely furnished apartments are the perfect environment for an Action Girl with a tortured past to dwell on her hideous, unforgivable acts of violence. Plus the hard, carpetless floors make cleaning up blood a breeze — whether it's your own blood from cutting yourself as self-punishment, or the blood of some random guy you brought home to hate-fuck to death.

Once I helped Beretta move into her very own bare bones abode, she was ready to start living her best life: curled up on the floor for days in a self-hatred induced coma!

FINISHING TOUCH: Every barely furnished apartment needs one deeply personal item that serves as a symbol for your entire tragic backstory. Maybe a music box that plays the song the government used to brainwash you, or a locket with a picture of your murdered sister in it. Whatever it is, be sure to keep it out in plain site then refuse to talk about it when anyone asks.

FILE #3

NAME: ALEXIS HART

OCCUPATION: **Housewife**

HOUSING CRISIS: Alexis was one of the top agents in the field, but the time had come for her to hang up her leather catsuit. I'm talking about Action Girl retirement age: her mid to late 20's! Let me tell you, she was sailing into enforced obsolescence with the whole package. A clueless husband with no idea about her secret agent past? CHECK! Two newborn baby twins who would only ever think of her as "Mom?" DOUBLE CHECK! Fifty more years of channeling her killer instinct into PTA bake sales and coaching her kids' soccer team? CHECK, CHECK and CHECK!

The only piece of the puzzle that was missing was her own little slice of suburbia. She had a lot to think about when picking out the perfect home – everything from land appreciation rates to proximity to good school districts. Unfortunately she wasn't asking herself the most important question every ex-Action Girl must ask when considering a new home... HOW EASILY WILL THIS HOUSE EXPLODE?!

HER PERFECT PLACE: **An easily explodable suburban house**

The safest place for any Action Girl with a new family is an easily explodable suburban house! Alexis was glad she took this advice when Dragon Shogun Assassin Squad came crashing into her kitchen just a few nights later. When those back-flipping bitches showed up, she couldn't have been happier with the easy to slice methane lines and cabinets full of loose matches I insisted upon.

By simply blowing up her entire house she was able to get rid of the Lady Dragons in a fraction of the time it would have taken her to call the police, or engage in a sword fight where she used a frying pan like a sword.

FINISHING TOUCH: A Surprisingly Sharp White Picket Fence. These icons of old school Americana will give your new home a cute, quaint and cozy vibe. Plus it will look super cool when an explosion flings someone into the air and they get impaled on one of the fence posts.

WMDs: *WEAPONS OF MASS DOMESTICATION*

Here a few essential items every Action Girl needs in her house or apartment, along with how they can be transformed into deadly weapons!

THE ESSENTIAL	THE WEAPON
WINE GLASSES: Set of twelve. Enough for entertaining.	**WEAPONIZED WINE GLASSES:** Keep a single wine glass lined with poison. Serve to your worst enemy – or to your boyfriend, Ben, when you find out he's an undercover S.T.A.B. Agent.
AREA RUG: A nice rug can really pull a room together.	**WEAPONIZED AREA RUG:** A nice rug can also be pulled out from under Ben when he realizes his wine glass was poisoned!
CUTLERY SET: An array of all-purpose knives...	**WEAPONIZED CUTLERY SET:** ...that you can purposely throw at Ben to knock that gun out of his hand!
COOKWARE: A sturdy set of pots and pans.	**WEAPONIZED COOKWARE:** Ben has a sword now! All you have is your skillet! Is it sturdy enough to stand up to the legendary Shashka Sabre?

THE ESSENTIAL	THE WEAPON
ART ON THE WALL: Something classy, in a nice frame.	*WEAPONIZED ART ON THE WALL:* **Smash Ben's smug face into the nice frame, over and over again!**
DECORATIVE TOWELS: Fluffy, colorful and absorbent!	*WEAPONIZED DECORATIVE TOWELS:* **Keep screaming, Ben, no one will ever hear you!**
CANDLES: They add atmosphere and aroma to your bathroom!	*WEAPONIZED CANDLES:* **Your pain is nothing compared to the searing pain of heartbreak. Why did you do this to us?**
WALK-IN CLOSET: Big enough to hold all your outfits...	*WEAPONIZED WALK-IN CLOSET:* **...and Ben for the indefinite future. He thought you were going to kill him? Oh no, tonight was just the foreplay. He doesn't get off that easy. This relationship is just getting started.**

GO FOR THE SKILL!

CLEAN START:
The ability to constantly start your life over everytime your cover is blown. (Hopefully you have a friend like Wesley in the tech department. He's always so excited to help me move!)

ETIQUETTE IN ACTION

Action Ladies of the past weren't liberated like we are today. If an Action Dude gave them a gun all they could do is ask where to point it and when to pull the trigger. When I think about all those awesome Action Girls who weren't granted the agency to realize their full, ass-kicking potential, I can only say one thing... *FREAKING LUCKY!*

Back then, we never had to ask what our role was. Back then, it was obvious. We were love interests! We were damsels in distress! We were pretty accessories who knew when to strip down to their skivvies, get captured and wait for a man to come set them free.

Today we have to be so much more...

I mean we still have to be love interests, damsels in distress and pretty accessories, but we have to be bold and empowered love interests, damsels in distress and pretty accessories. That's why Action Etiquette is more important today than ever before. Without it, we risk crossing the razor-thin line from self-assured but likable female hero into overconfident bitch.

That's why I've put together a list of the most common code of conduct conundrums you will face in your day-to-day life as an Action Girl. So pay attention, play along and always remember: just because you save the world doesn't mean you should act like it owes you anything.

MAN HANDLED

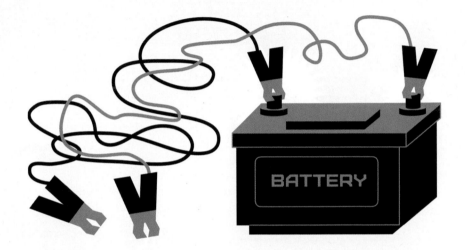

SCENARIO: **A male agent has been kidnapped, tied up and tortured by a bunch of bad guys. You're there to rescue him! But the only thing worse than a shock to a guy's testicles is a shock to his ego.**

THE DILEMMA: How can you save him without emasculating him?

THE SOLUTION: Fight like a girl! You can totally assert yourself physically, so long as you do it in the most feminine way possible. When you start kicking bad guy butt throw in lots of high kicks, splits and thigh squeezing. Think of yourself as a high-class stripper and your enemies as a bunch of evil, sentient stripper poles that you need to murder with your hot body. If you brought a gun, put it away – even if it would make the job a little easier. The guy you're saving probably had a gun when he got captured, so he's going to feel really bad if he sees you using one proficiently. Do it right and your male agent won't feel like he's being rescued. He'll feel like he's enjoying a sexy little show only for him.

SCENARIO: **You've been captured by eco-terrorist Gideon Blaze, and he wants to exchange you for the Inferno Virus.**

THE DILEMMA: Should you plead for your life or accept your fate?

THE SOLUTION: Accept your fate! Any Action Girl worth her running pumps is always willing to suck it up and die for a cause. But here's the fun catch – an Action Guy will never actually let you die! They're psychologically programmed to think anything other than 100% success is a complete failure. That means if they save the world but lose you it will haunt them for the rest of their lives. It's an emotional handicap you can totally take advantage of! So just work up some tears, start to quiver and shout stuff like "Don't do it! Don't give him the virus! Just let me die!" You'll look noble and brave and he'll be having a psychotic meltdown trying to figure out how to save you! Yay!

SELFISH FULFILLING PROPHECY

SCENARIO: **You and a male agent have just broken into TechCorp Industries and discovered the NanoAmulet (the amulet that will grant its wearer all the powers of the digital world).**

THE DILEMMA: You both want the NanoAmulet, but he says that he needs it to fulfill the Cyber Prophecy. (Note: the Cyber Prophecy does not mention sharing.)

THE SOLUTION: In most cases, just caving into a man would be considered a weak move,

but this is a unique situation, since he really thinks he deserves this. Guys love to fulfill prophecies. Just look at it from his perspective. He's gone his whole life being told he needs to embrace his destiny as the Cyber King and drive all the Holo-Beasts back to the Digi-Realm. Now you come along and tell him that maybe he doesn't deserve all that? That's pretty shitty. You don't want to be the girl who tells a guy he's not as important as the world says he is. (If you do, he'll totally harass you on social media.)

SCENARIO: **A dimensional rift has opened and the Hell Spawn are invading downtown Minneapolis. You've joined an elite squad of heroes, each with your own special set of skills, to drive them back into the rift. But oh no, there's already another girl on the team!**

THE DILEMMA: How can you have two girls on one team?!

THE SOLUTION: Proper action etiquette dictates that any team of heroes is only allowed to add one woman for every four men.

It's why all four-person teams are strictly male. At minimum, guys need a buffer of four other guys before they can deal with another woman. So just be patient, and wait for more men to join the team! You may not be able to jump in on this particular adventure, but if it's successful there's sure to be another one right around the corner, and along with it will come a bunch of brand new cool and colorful male heroes... and you: the second acceptable female! (For more on this, see page 50.)

CHANGING RELATIONSHIPS

THE SCENARIO: **Maybe he was bitten by a werewolf or a vampire. Maybe his blood was contaminated with alien DNA and he's becoming a human-xentrapede hybrid. Whatever it is, every Action Girl will eventually end up in a relationship where her boyfriend starts transforming into a boyfreak!**

THE DILEMMA: Do you stand by your man, no matter what he becomes?

THE SOLUTION: DUMP HIM! Guys who transform into monsters also transform into needy, high-maintenance time sucks. I've seen it happen to way too many of my girlfriends. Their boyfriend's promise them that, just because their body is now 85% synthetic they won't love them any less. Then, just a few days later, they're missing date nights and giving lame excuses about how you can't understand what they're going through, you can't understand what it feels like to have all this power. We understand that it turns you into a jerk!

THE SCENARIO: **You know that top secret government defense agency that recruited you when you were just a kid? Well it turns out they've been secretly siphoning your blood in your sleep for the last sixteen years to get access to the Kratos Serum! (So that's what your scientist-mother meant when she said, "the Kratos Serum will always be a part of you!")**

THE DILEMMA: Do you let Admiral Zorn know it wasn't cool to steal your super blood without asking, or do you just let it go?

THE SOLUTION: If you have super blood, people will try to steal it, that's just a fact of life. The important thing is that they steal your blood while still respecting you. You don't have to put them on blast, just let them know next time they want your super blood you'd like to be asked first, because in most cases, you'd be fine with it. Especially if they're using your super blood to engineer a team of secret agent super insects; including Spy-Dar (the eight-legged leader), Beetle Brawler (the strong-bug with an attitude as tough as his exoskeleton) and Pray-Pray (the sassy hacker mantis).

TEAM DYNAMIC

Whether we're talking superheroes or spies, marines or monster hunters, the gender politics of Action Teams can get confusing. How do you know when it's your turn to be recruited?

FOUR GUYS ON TEAM:
FIRST FEMALE ALLOWED TO JOIN:
The first girl is just "the girl," so don't worry about having any compelling character traits beside your boobs and vagina. You should be very prone to crossing your arms, rolling your eyes and saying "boys will be boys" whenever the boys do something really boyish (which they're always doing! They're boys!). And OMG, lucky you: You automatically get to be the team leader's love interest! Romance is so easy when you don't have a choice!

EIGHT GUYS ON TEAM:
SECOND FEMALE ALLOWED TO JOIN
The second girl on the team gets to act more like one of the guys, since all the main girl-sponsibilites are imposed on the first girl. You can even drink a beer with them and imply that the first girl is stuck up for not drinking beer! However, the second girl must have some minor eccentricities. Maybe she's got a sense of humor. Maybe she has a short haircut. Maybe she isn't even white. She's gotta distinguish herself from the main girl on the team!

TWELVE GUYS ON TEAM:

REFORMED FEMALE VILLAIN ALLOWED TO JOIN

A reformed female villain will distinguish herself nicely from the two "good girls" by being "not good." Reformed female villains tend to be added reluctantly, entering into an uneasy truce with the team. This will prevent the guys looking weak for adding a third girl, so long as they constantly remind her that the only reason she's still alive is because they need her.

ANYTHING OVER TWELVE GUYS:

STOP ADDING FEMALES

Listen, after twelve guys, you can't add any more girls. Space is just too tight! At this point, the original female team members have been on at least two adventures, which means their usefulness has expired – and *they* should too! If you were the first girl, bow out with dignity by dying in the saddest way possible, to be replaced by an all-new girl who will get her chance to die too, very soon!

ALL FEMALE TEAMS:

ADD ALL THE FEMALES

While rare, all-female action teams do exist. When you are added to one of these teams, try not to fight over who gets to be the sexy one. JK! You all get to be the sexy one!

QUIZ: *SHOULD I SPIT IN THE BAD GUY'S FACE?*

Spitting in the bad guy's face is a bold move. Next time you want to spit in the bad guy's face, take this quick quiz to determine if you should.

1. How tied up are you?

A) Not tied up.

B) Tied up but I could probably break out.

C) Super tied up! In a room full of pipes and steam!

2. How close are you to the bad guy?

A) He's a few feet away.

B) He's a few inches away.

C) So close I can see my reflection in his glasses (or monocle).

3. Is spitting your only option?

A) No, I have a gun... they spit bullets.

B) I think he's close enough to get a headbutt in.

C) Spit is the only thing that will convey my utter contempt for him.

4. How much spit do you have built up?

A) A little bit of spittle.

B) A mouthful of saliva.

C) I could get a pretty sweet loogie hanging from his cheek.

5. Why do you want to spit in his face?

A) He's the man who killed my sister.

B) Once he pushes that button... it's World War Three.

C) He's stroking my face and saying he has "plans" for me.

6. Is he basically taunting you to spit in his face?

A) No. How dare you?

B) No one shows Colonel Yune such disrespect and lives to tell the tale.

C) This creep totally wants spit in his face.

7. How do you think he'll react?

A) He'll explode into an indignant rage.

B) He'll tell his men to teach me some manners.

C) He'll lovingly wipe it off his face and taste it.

8. Does this dude want spit in his face?

A) Prubably.

B) It feels like he's asking for it.

C) Yeah... I think it might be like, a sex thing.

RESULTS: **Oh you want to know the result of this quiz? Why don't you come a in a little bit closer, so I can whisper it in your ear? *PTOO!* Ha! I'll take the results of this quiz to the grave!**

CHAPTER FIVE

DATING ON THIN ICE

An Action Girl can only settle for nitro-charged one night stands for so long. Sooner or later, she has to start looking for something a little more meaningful. Otherwise she's on a bullet train to spinsterhood, complete with an apartment full of cats, all named after the warlords and dictators she's killed. But how do you do it? How do you find Mr. Perfect in a world full of guys who are more likely to be looking for the Kratos Serum than true love?

The answer is the same thing Wesley down in the tech department told me when I was fighting those assassins equipped with Chameleon-flage (the camouflage serum made from chameleon DNA!) "KEEP YOUR EYES OPEN! Love always strikes when you least expect it. It could even be in front of you right now, stealthily blending in with a brick wall or the passenger side seat of your car. If a girl isn't constantly on her guard, the love of her life could slip by without you ever realizing." (Wesley literally said all that. It seemed slightly off topic, but Wesley is such goof. He's like my best friend.)

Potential date material is everywhere! So in this chapter, we're going to take a look at some of the best places to make a love connection. Be cautious: you shouldn't sign up for life-long missions of love and commitment with just anybody. That's why we'll also take a look at the types of guys you should go after versus the types of guys you should secretly poison once they take their eyes off their drink.

DATING APPS

Today's dating apps make meeting people so simple, and it makes lying to them even easier! I've created dozens of different dating profiles for my various secret identities. Who will I be tonight? Maybe Melanie Grant, hot shot lady lawyer from London? Or Haley Hartstone, small town girl and bar owner from Beaufort? So long as the guy swiping right has got the goods, I don't care! If you want to build a relationship on an elaborate web of lies, a dating app is the perfect place to start.

GUYS TO GO FOR: Good-natured dolts / Kind-hearted stooges / Dreamy dummies who won't suspect anything about your secret identity.

GUYS TO AVOID: Master Hacker, Simon Warlock.

BEST APPS: Findr/Cindr/Snatch.com/Any app that sounds familiar, but not "copyright" familiar.

WORST APPS: HackMatch (the app that matches you up with the evil hacker of your dreams).

It may seem cliche, but nightclubs are still one of the best places to meet guys who are being blackmailed by shadowy organizations. Whenever a cute yet helpless hunk has to meet face to face with people who are destroying his life, he's going to do it in a shadowy, smoke-filled club where the techno music is blasting at full volume.

GUYS TO GO FOR: Cute district attorneys getting blackmailed by the mob/Cute nuclear physicists turning over blueprints for the Omega Drive.

GUYS TO AVOID: Club Vampires (Vampires who open nightclubs as traps to lure in young victims. If fifty or sixty kids go missing in your city every weekend, it's probably because of Club Vampires).

BEST CLUBS: Cross Fyre, Hot Wyre, Inspyre (Any club that spells its name with a "y" where an "i" should be is pretty cool).

WORST CLUBS: Club Fang/The Blood Faucet/Vampyre Zone/The Human Trap.

HIJACKED *PLANES, TRAINS OR BUSES*

There's no better breeding ground for romance than the tight quarters and extreme stress of a high-speed vehicle hurtling towards disaster. Plus, it's the perfect place to meet the the Action Girl Dream Man: an average Joe who steps up and takes charge. There is nothing hotter than some random dude with no training, no skills and no authority who risks his life, and the lives of countless others, to look like a big hero.

GUYS TO GO FOR: Retired marines/Vacationing cops/Ex-soldiers who are "just trying to get home."

GUYS TO AVOID: Bradley! That weasel thinks we should just play ball with the terrorists. But I've got news for you, Bradley: These terrorists aren't American... they don't play ball.

BEST VEHICLES: Anything that also happens to be transporting a convicted war criminal or deadly weapon in the cargo hold.

WORST VEHICLES: Bradley's new Lamborghini. You really think the terrorists will let you go in exchange for your fancy sports car, Bradley? YOU'RE GOING TO GET US ALL KILLED!

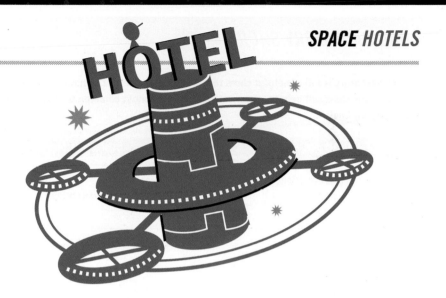

Cosmic ray cocktails! Dancing amongst the stars! Zero-G bed chambers! Nothing's more romantic than a mission to one of the many Outer Space Hotels orbiting Earth. Next time you and Wesley from the tech department get assigned to uncover the mystery of who's trying to assassinate the Galactic Prime Minister, take some time to look for love. Even Wesley looks cute in all this moonlight.

GUYS TO GO FOR: Any of the millionaire bachelor playboys who are known to frequent space hotels. And maybe Wesley... no, no... he's just a friend.... Right...?

GUYS TO AVOID: The galactic prime minister! He hired those assassins! He's trying to start the galactic civil war with Earth! I guess that's what we get for electing a filthy Cybropod.

BEST SPACE HOTELS: I mean, they're hotels in outer space. They're all pretty great.

WORST SPACE HOTELS: Space hotels! Don't start complaining about space hotels. Men get really insecure when they think you don't like your space hotel.

LONG BACKSTORY SHORT

A guy's backstory is full of helpful clues that will betray whether or not he's boyfriend material. This chart will help you translate some of the most common backstory phrases into everyday English.

WHAT HE SAYS:	WHAT HE MEANS:
"I lost everything that day... and everyone."	**Available!!!!!**
"There was just one design flaw... they gave me a soul."	**I'm a really nice guy.** **AKA:** **BOOORING!**
"No one had to teach me how to kill... I picked that up all on my own."	**Bad boy alert!**
"I would do anything to get rid of these powers... anything!"	**I'm willing to change for you.**
"I lived with her for three years... and in all that time I never realized she was The Leap Year Killer."	**I'm still not over my ex.**
"Judge me all you want... but I did what I had to in order to survive."	**My dick has all of the STDs.**

WHAT HE SAYS:	WHAT HE MEANS:
"I still sometimes wonder whatever happened to her... she'd be just about the same age as you now."	**I'm probably your dad.**
"That throne is my birthright... but I will never sit on it until I reclaim the Sword of Gonthore."	**I'm unemployed.**
"My homeworld may be gone, but I know there are others of my kind out there... and I will find them!"	**Bros before hoes.**
"Let's just say I work for a delivery service up North... way up north!"	**I'm actually Santa Claus and I'm on an undercover mission for the Council of Holidays. Tonight I'm going to kill the Krampus once and for all.**
"Oh, my childhood was nothing special. I grew up in a web... I MEAN A HOUSE! A COMPLETELY NORMAL HUMAN HOUSE!"	**I'm actually a member of B.U.G. Force controlling an extremely lifelike human animatron. (There's a little cockpit in the head!)**

GO FOR THE SKILL!

SEXPOSITION:

The ability to deliver boring exposition in the sexiest way possible in order to keep everyone alert and interested.

BLAH BLAH BLAH

INTERCOURSE OF ACTION

Battling a bunch of bad guys in hand-to-hand combat is a great way to get to know a potential love interest. It can also be a great way for them to get to know how good you are at sex. There are tons of awesome, field-tested moves that will bring down your enemies while subtly hinting at your skills under the covers. Consider this your very own Combat Sutra!

The Hungry Mantis.
STEP 1: Wrap enemy's head in thighs.
STEP 2: Squeeze until you hear a sexy snap!

COMBAT *SUTRA*

The Grasping Claw
STEP 1: Firmly grasp shaft of enemy's gun with both hands.
STEP 2: Stroke vigorously until enemy releases weapon.

The Grazing Camel
STEP 1: Stand directly in line of fire.
STEP 2: Arch spine backwards so breasts are in full display.
STEP 3: Allow bullets to safely graze over your nipples.

The Snapping Crab
STEP 1: Grab enemy by crotch.
STEP 2: Squeeze hard enough that it hurts, but in a way that if you did it like 15% less hard, would probably feel really good.

The Flashing Windmill
STEP 1: Allow enemies to form circle around you.
STEP 2: Raise one leg over your head.
STEP 3: Face kick all enemies in a single twirl.
STEP4: After enemies have fallen, leave leg raised long enough to give everyone a decent view.

The Writhing Serpent
STEP 1: Find room guarded by web of deadly red lasers.
STEP 2: Slither through deadly lasers.
STEP 3: Get butt as close to deadly lasers as possible.

The Coiled Rattlesnake

"witty comment"

STEP 1: Wrap legs around enemy's waist.
STEP 2: Wait until enemy is fully erect.

STEP 3: Engage in intercourse with enemy.
STEP 4: A couple of times, if you want.
STEP 5: Let enemy divulge top secret information as he falls asleep cuddled next to you.

STEP 6: Strangle enemy to death with garrote wire hidden in your necklace.
STEP 7: Say something witty like, "What's the matter... I thought you said you liked it *rough*?"

THE FIEND ZONE

Oops! You had sex with a bad guy! It happens. You obviously need to break it off without hurting his feelings. Here's what you can say to spare a bad guy's pride.

EVIL DICTATOR: You're working on your evil empire, I'm working on myself. It's probably just a bad time for the both of us.

KILLER ROBOT: I just got out of a long-term relationship with a sentient computer and I'm not looking to date another death machine right now.

DRUG KINGPIN: Your career is just about to take off. You don't want me around to distract you from developing the next Super-Crack or Ultra-Heroin.

SHADOW NINJA: You spend so much time in the shadows, I just feel like we'd never actually see each other.

CORPSE MONSTER: I just think of you like my brother... 's corpse, stitched together with a bunch of other corpses and brought back to life in defiance of God's law.

CULT LEADER: I'm Jewish. I don't want to make you convert and stop worshiping The Ancient Ones.

ALIEN WARLORD: We're from two different worlds! Get it?!

ILLEGAL ARMS DEALER: I wouldn't feel safe having kids with someone who's gonna leave railguns lying around the house.

SERIAL KILLER: I'm not right for you. You deserve a girl whose skin you would look good wearing.

TIME TRAVELING RASPUTIN: You're not in love with me. I'm just the first girl you saw after the Czar threw you into that time vortex.

BARON VON COCKROACH: I'm just not interested. But you know Pray-Pray, from B.U.G. Force? I heard her talking about you. You should call her.

VAMPIRE/WEREWOLF/ETC: Oh coooool... I'd love to date you! Unless you know of any literal piles of garbage that I could date. Hahahaha! Get real, you supernatural nerds!

BASE INSTINCT

Action Girls are regularly trapped in dangerously out-of-control buses, hijacked airplanes and spaceships re-entering the atmosphere. Why also get trapped in a bad relationship?!

Of course, that's easier said than done! How are you not supposed to develop feelings for the man you're on a mission with? Tensions are high, the air is electric, knives are constantly being thrown into walls just inches from your head. Unfortunately, those same spur-of-the-moment feelings are also going to blind you to everything wrong with him. For example, did you know that most Action Guys...

- Are two to three decades older than most Action Girls?
- Have dozens of ex-girlfriends, most of whom are dead?
- Are kind of paunchy?

I've fallen into bad relationships with too many of these losers, and I won't let it happen again. Neither should you! There are stages to relationships; bases that every Action Girl should hit on the road to finally settling down. You need to go through these with every potential paramour, whether he's a suave spy, manly marine or a guy from the tech department who you're maybe starting to see something special in.

FIRST *DATE*

X-TREME CROSSING

First dates are all about cutting to the chase – literally! An adrenaline-pumping chase sequence is a great way for two people to get to know each other. It's active, it's fun and you're so focused on escaping the thing trying to kill you that you don't have time to obsess over everything going perfectly. It's easy to be yourself when impending doom is just a few footsteps away.

GREAT DATES: Parkour run over the rooftops of London/Backwards car chase through the streets of Paris/Frantic escape from a pack of genetically modified ape-men.

HE SHOULD: Try to hold your hand.

YOU SHOULD: Run ahead and tell him to "keep up."

BASE JUMP: For a first date never go over first base: a single kiss before you slip away into the night, giving him no way to contact you.

Second dates are the perfect time for your first fight. No, not with each other! With a bunch of easily defeatable goons! Taking on a bunch of easily defeatable goons will give you a good idea about how sustainable your chemistry is. When you two are handcuffed back to back, does he spin you around so you can use your legs as weapons? Or do you two just argue about how to get uncuffed? When you tell him you don't need his help, does he shoot the bad guy sneaking up behind you and give you a cute smile? Or does he let the bad guy get the drop on you just to prove a point? If the fight is fun, breezy and filled with witty banter, then you may have a keeper on your hands.

GREAT DATES: Breaking into a weapons compound / Breaking into a ninja lair / Breaking into Principal Doomslayer's office.

HE SHOULD: Let you knock out at least one goon.

YOU SHOULD: Let him fight the main goon.

BASE JUMP: A little more physical contact is ok for a second date. Let him shield you from an explosion with his body. BONUS: it'll totally show you how good a snuggler he is.

THIRD *DATE*

It's your third date and time to go undercover. Whoa, whoa, whoa: don't get ahead of me here, girls! Not undercover as in "under the covers." I mean undercover as in an undercover mission. (Although if the undercover mission has you posing as a married couple, you will have to go under the covers.) Pretending to be a different couple is a fun way to strengthen the bond you two are already developing. Nothing connects two people faster than being the only ones who know each other's true identity. It's like a fun little secret that could get you killed.

GREAT DATES: Crash an evil dictator's wedding in the Alps/Infiltrate a company retreat for the families of the SinTech Industries.

HE SHOULD: Pick out a dress for you and say, "I think you'd look good in this."

YOU SHOULD: Look good in that dress.

BASE JUMP: You guys have waited long enough, time for your first make out sesh. But wait for the perfect moment, like when a henchman finds you in a restricted area and you need to look like you only went in there to fuck.

Alright, four dates in, time to see if he can really bring the fireworks. Hold on – I don't mean emotional fireworks! Well actually, yes, at this point there should be emotional fireworks. But I also mean actual fireworks, LIKE EXPLOSIONS! The fourth date is when you two should outrun your first fireball together! Simply find your favorite long hallway, decommissioned airfield or warehouse full of old oil drums and run... for love!

GREAT DATES: Blowing up an enemy satellite dish/Outrunning the rear exhaust of a jet that you two just barely manage to escape.

HE SHOULD: Try to take your hand.

YOU SHOULD: Let him have it this time!

BASE JUMP: Your bodies dripping with sweat. Half your clothes singed off. Flaming rubble lighting up the night sky. The mood is right for you two to finally give in and go all the way.

FIFTH *DATE*

OK! Here it is. Date Number Five! This one's for all the money on the table. And by all the money on the table I mean the literal money that you're being ransomed for, because this is the date where you should get yourself captured. (Also by "money you're being ransomed for" I don't mean actual money. I mean, it could be actual money, but it could also be an experimental weapon, or something. Whatever, you get it!) If this really is the guy that you're going to build a long and lasting relationship with, then you need to see if he comes running when you get kidnapped.

GREAT DATES: Tied to a bomb/Tied to the mast of a battleship/Tied to anything really.

HE SHOULD: Do everything in his power to save you.

YOU SHOULD: Do nothing! Let him take the lead on this one!

BASE JUMP: Slow down. If he tries to put the moves on you after the trauma of being captured he's a jerk! Kick him to the curb!

If you two are going to be together forever, there can be no secrets between you. That's why, before you make it official, he must tell you his *dark secret*. Every Action Guy has one, and it's up to you to decide if it's one you can live with. If his dark secret is something minor, like he shot a child he thought was trying to assassinate the President, then you two will have a happy future together. If his dark secret is more complex, like he's not really a guy from the tech department but actually a super advanced human animatron being controlled by a member of B.U.G. Force, then it's time to cut ties and move on.

GREAT DATES: Anything in public, so he doesn't make a scene if you dump him on the spot.

HE SHOULD: Understand that it's not that you don't like bugs, it's just that B.U.G. force was created from your blood, so getting together would feel kind of incesty.

YOU SHOULD: Not give into the very understandable desire to fuck a member of B.U.G. Force.

GO FOR THE SKILL!

THE AGE GAP:

The most important skill for any Action Girl to master? Being between 22 and 29!

JOAN HAVOC
AGE: Twenties-ish

QUIZ: *JERK OR BURN NOTICED?*

Is your new guy distant because he's a jerk or because he's an ex-spy about to be exterminated by the government agency he betrayed? Let's see what's up!

1. When you tell him you've had a bad day, he says...

A) You think your day was bad! Wait till you hear about mine!

B) Jeeze! You had another bad day. Big surprise!

C) I want to hear all about it... away from the open window.

2. Your friends' biggest complaint about your boyfriend is..

A) He's always flirting with them.

B) He never picks up the check.

C) He uses them for sniper cover.

3. If he catches another guy making eyes at you, he will...

A) Start a fight with the guy.

B) Tell the guy that you're taken.

C) Stare at the guy with his weird beeping sunglasses. Wait for sunglasses to say, "SCAN COMPLETE. NO THREAT DETECTED."

4. It's date night! Dinner and dancing (your choice) or a baseball game (his choice)?

A) Take me out to the ballgame... bleh.

B) We flip for it.

C) Sudden change of plans! How about a romantic trip to the mountains? Which mountains? Any mountains! It doesn't matter! Let's just go!

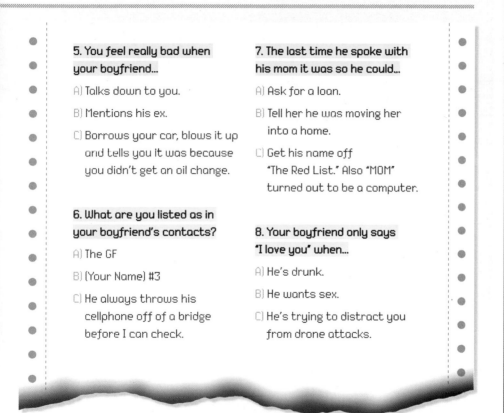

5. You feel really bad when your boyfriend...

A) Talks down to you.

B) Mentions his ex.

C) Borrows your car, blows it up and tells you it was because you didn't get an oil change.

6. What are you listed as in your boyfriend's contacts?

A) The GF

B) (Your Name) #3

C) He always throws his cellphone off of a bridge before I can check.

7. The last time he spoke with his mom it was so he could...

A) Ask for a loan.

B) Tell her he was moving her into a home.

C) Get his name off "The Red List." Also "MOM" turned out to be a computer.

8. Your boyfriend only says "I love you" when...

A) He's drunk.

B) He wants sex.

C) He's trying to distract you from drone attacks.

RESULTS: **Listen, we want to give you the results, we really do. It's just... well... the results are going to make things with your boyfriend complicated, and you're the only uncomplicated thing in his life.**

IT'S NOT THE END OF THE WORLD
[JUST THE END OF THIS BOOK]

Well Action Girls, it looks like we've reached the end of your training. Now comes the scariest part of any mission. The part where you have to go it alone. Just know that if you're ever feeling outnumbered, outgunned or way out of your league, don't freak out! This book has one last, never fail trick that will get you out of any situation, no matter how sticky:

SET THIS BOOK ON FIRE AND THROW IT AT YOUR ENEMIES! The cheap-o paper stock we used is super flammable and will burn a bad guy to death in seconds.

Before you set this book on fire, I hope that it's taught you a few things about yourself. Maybe it taught you that us girls have everything we need to take the lead in our own adventures. Maybe it taught you that Admiral Zorn is actually your father and he used your super blood to create an army of super bugs. Or maybe, just maybe, it taught you how to reshape your entire appearance and personality to gain the approval of others.

And yeah, I know what you're thinking... again! "Joan, how am I supposed to be a tough, independent, modern-day Action Girl while still conforming to society's regressive standards for the female gender? Isn't that impossible? Isn't the whole premise of this book wildly contradictory?"

KILLING IT

THE ACTION GIRLS' GUIDE TO SAVING THE WORLD

WHILE LOOKING HOT!

JOAN FORD

SHUT UP... AGAIN!

Sure, it may seem impossible, but when did "impossible" ever stop us? What makes an Action Girl an Action Girl is her ability to wriggle through these contradictions like a laser grid protecting the crown jewels, the constitution, and the Mona Lisa in some sort of super museum!

It takes a special kind of girl to keep her nails glossy, her makeup flawless, never pussing out with a pair of flats. Who doesn't mind being seduced by a man she just slapped across the face fifteen minutes ago? Who's ready to say "Hey world! I'm cool, confident and competent, but not so much that it makes anyone uncomfortable?" It takes an *Action Girl*.

At the end of the day, that's all you have to remember. Plus, everything else in this book. And don't forget all the other unwritten social mandates women are tacitly expected to follow at all times. If you can remember all that, you'll be...

...KILLING IT!

ACKNOWLEDGEMENTS

This book came together when an elite team of comedy pros all agreed to one last mission. Thank you to the Devastator Author Corps, who helped line these pages with enough jokes to blow up a three whole city blocks. Thank you to Asterios Kokkinos, who re-coded the entire mainframe to ensure this book was running at 120% processing capacity. And thank you to Devastator Masterminds, Amanda and Geoffrey, who are making the world safe for print comedy one funny book at a time.

ABOUT THE AUTHOR

JOAN FORD is a writer who lives on the edge of darkness, which is in Los Angeles. She is a regular performer at The Upright Citizens Brigade Theatre and her work has been featured on a bunch of websites her parents have never heard of. She's seen a lot of action movies in her life and in her opinion, every *Die Hard* film should take place on Christmas Eve.

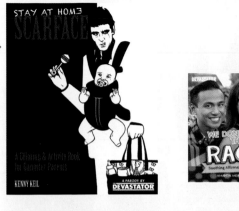